For Maureen,
    When i saw this today... it had your name on it — talking about the way things ask to be reached for. — Something especially sacred about the pictures — maybe the gentle answer of how Adam can finally touch God.

Peace, and many rebornings

Dana

Please Touch

Please Touch

EDWIN M. McMAHON
PETER A. CAMPBELL

 A SEARCH BOOK published by Sheed and Ward

The quotation from Antoine de Saint Exupéry
Wind, Sand and Stars: New York, Harcourt,
Brace & World, Inc., (Harbrace Paperback
Library) 1967, is used by permission of the
publisher.

All biblical quotations used in this book are from
The New English Bible, New Testament, © The
Delegates of the Oxford University Press and
The Syndics of the Cambridge University Press
1961.

To Our Friends in Canada

We think of religious activity
   as directed toward God
                        —instead of man.

We believe in someone divine
   rather than in ourselves.

Maybe we have turned religion
   inside-out.

A famous Japanese sculptor
once confounded the curators
of an American art gallery
where his works were being shown.

At the base of each statue
the sculptor had placed
a polite little sign.

The signs all read:

"PLEASE TOUCH"

Can we turn "touching" inside-out
to find man—
and God?

Touching is wonder.
   We think of it as reaching *out*
      to know
         to grow
            to explore
               to love
                  to believe.
But there is also reaching
   within . . .
an inside touching that comes first.

"Satori" is the Zen way
   of acquiring a new point of view
      for living
and looking.
   Not creating something new—
      but seeing
and touching
   in a different way.
It approaches religion
   from the inside
      letting it emerge
from man
   rather than being imposed.
It finds
   a revelation of the divine
      within human experience,
within life itself.

People really want to believe
in themselves and one another.

This is "Revelation."

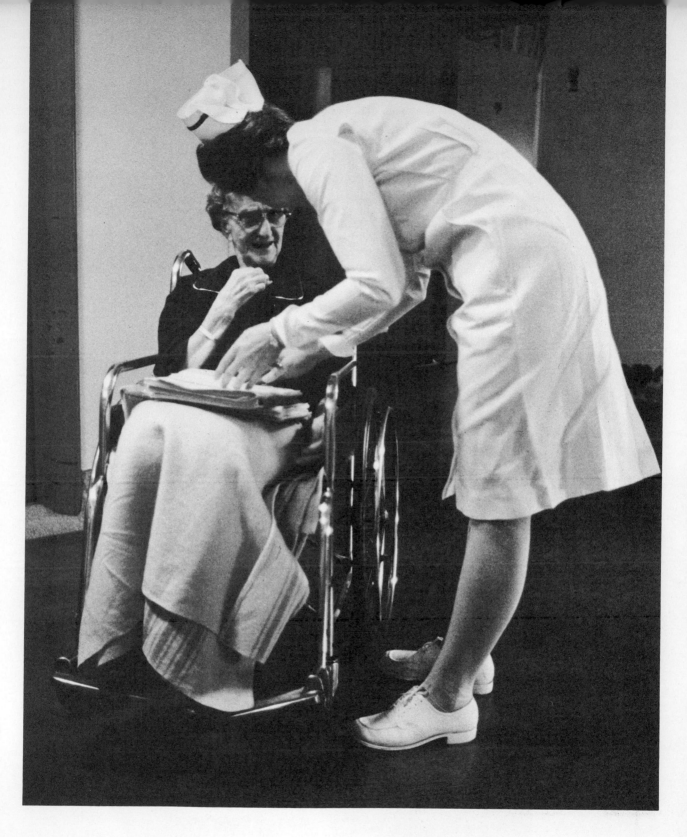

4

A shape
a form
a powerful voice
speaking from inside
the rough-hewn marble
of human experience.

"THE GLORY OF GOD IS MAN FULLY ALIVE."
—*St. Irenaeus of Lyons.*

What is required
    to approach human aliveness
        for what it really is—

Believing enough in ourselves
    to risk touching God-with-us
        as our experience
of trying to live a fully human life?

5

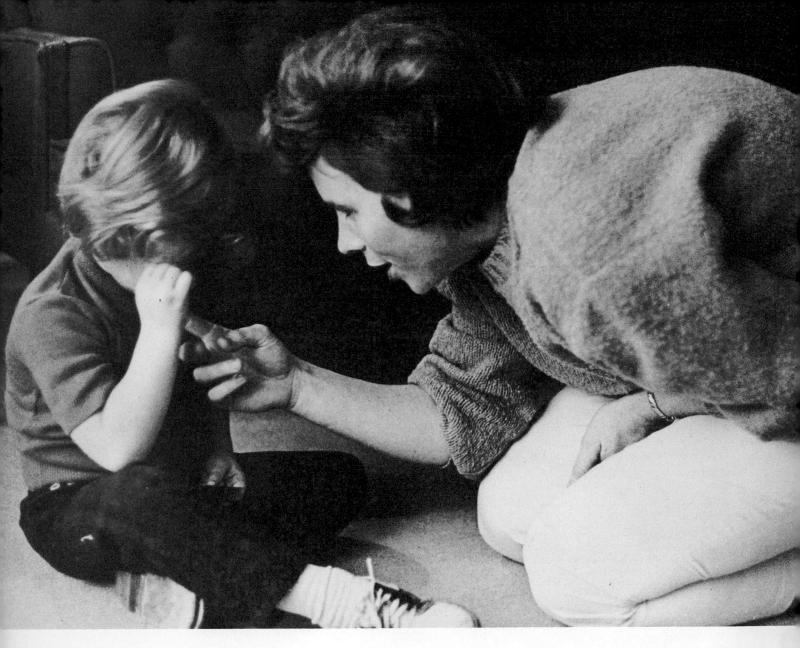

We do not come to believe in ourselves
until someone reveals that deep inside us
    something is
      valuable
worth listening to
    worthy of our trust
      sacred to our touch.

Spirit
  comes alive
when we are made alive
    by love.

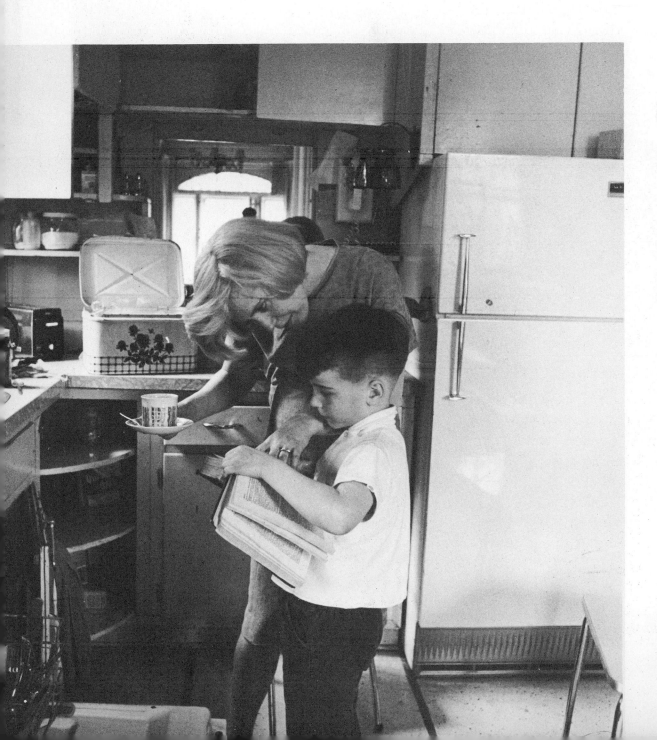

Spirit ebbs away
    with love's decline.

                    Such a fragile thing—
                        this life-love-force in a child.
                            Easily blunted—
                    Dulled
                        by poverty
                            disease
                                ignorance.

                        How terrible
                            to see the light
                                go out of a child's eyes,
                        to feel defensive stiffness
                            growing
                                in hunched little shoulders,
                        sensing mistrust
                            and calculated distance
                                being woven into the fabric
                                    of a fresh new life.

Once we believe in ourselves
we can risk
curiosity . . .
wonder . . .

11

... spontaneous delight

or any experience
that reveals
the human spirit

13

Hills can be obstacles
or
glorious delight.

When a child asks about God,
   what God do we name?

Someone "up there". . .?
   an invisible person . . .?

Why not answer with
   the experience of love
     wonder
       creativity
that invites children
   to discover something new
     in themselves
       for
whatever opens us
   to become more human
     is flesh
of the God we can know.

We strive to believe
   in an invisible personal God—
     searching with our minds alone
not knowing
   how to let our whole self
     touch
the incarnate God-with-us.

We "think" God into experiences
   to make them prayerful.

Instead of asking:
   "How should I pray?"
    we should ask:
"How can I grow?"
   How do I touch
     what is most real in myself
       and others—

       That something
         which ties us into the world
         and life?

How do we open out
   to a sight
     a touch
       a whisper of joy
   up
     and
       down
          the spine—
Drawing these
   into our faith-experience
     of God-with-us?

Why not let life itself
   teach us how to pray?
     Developing a "feel for life"
is
     developing a "feel for God."

This is indeed good to hear—
   the good news.

". . . to seek God, and, it might be, touch and find him; though indeed he is not far from each one of us, for in him we live and move, in him we exist." (Acts 17:27–28)

"... to seek God and, it might be,
touch and find him ..."

To let the forest get inside
    without thinking about
        what is happening—

Letting the mind go clear,
    resting in the enclosure
        of awesome silence.

Held,
    penetrated,
        invaded,
until the odor of needles
    and moist earth,
the gentle sound of a falling cone
    or droning insect
        in a beam of light
speak from deep inside
        you.

Called by spaciousness—
    feeling caught up within the sweep
        of soaring lines—
summoned—
    drawn out.

18

19

To pause
opened by delicate odors—
by patterned morning freshness.

20

To let your eye
    take you
        climbing
        and
    twisting
        along dark
        branches.

To breathe deep
    the sound
       the smell
          the feel
of water . . .

               To be
                  inside
                     never again
               the same.

We cannot touch—or even name—
　　God-with-us
　　apart from our experience of a world
　　　　that is "charged with the grandeur of
　　　　　　God."
Every moment of every day
　　fleshes the divine presence.

God touches us
　　in the same way that the world
　　　　and other people
touch us—

Calling,
　　inviting us
　　　　to become more open,
to become more human.

If we answer with all we are—
　　and hope to be—
　　　　then to live
is to live in faith
　　that we have found
　　　　and are at one with
an incarnate God.

The meadow is not God
　　you are not God
　　　　the patterned morning freshness
is not God.

But to open yourself to meadow and morning,
　　to what is before you
　　is to find *Emmanuel*, to know
God-with-us
　　as life in the moment.

*"All that came to be was alive with
his life, and that life was the
light of men." (John 1:4)*

We know this
　　in moments of beauty . . .

And yet,
    isolation and loneliness,
        greed
    suspicion, hate
        are experiences around us—
and within us—
    evil everywhere mingled
        with the beautiful.

Can we let deep human longing
    to overcome such evil
        get inside us too—?
as invitation?
    like light?
        space?
            color?
                sound?

The needs of others
    call us to be life-source
        finding light in the dark,
in sparks of human goodness
    alive
        beneath encrusted surfaces.

Can we so communicate belief
    in the basic goodness
        of people
that they come to believe
    in themselves—?
        mutually discovering
that
    "the light shines on in the dark . . ."

"... and the darkness has never
   quenched it." (John 1:5)

We must learn
   to celebrate life
      where we find it.

"I have come that men may have
life, and may have it in all
its fullness." (John 10:10)

"... because I live, you too will
   live ..." (John 14:19)

Believing enough in ourselves
   to celebrate
     God-with-us
Believing enough
   to say
    yes
to becoming more a person.

25

"THE GLORY OF GOD IS MAN
FULLY ALIVE."

Turning the energies
    of sinew and spirit
       toward expressing
what is good
    and sacred for us—

Really to
    "be me"
       in a way that liberates
       and humanizes.

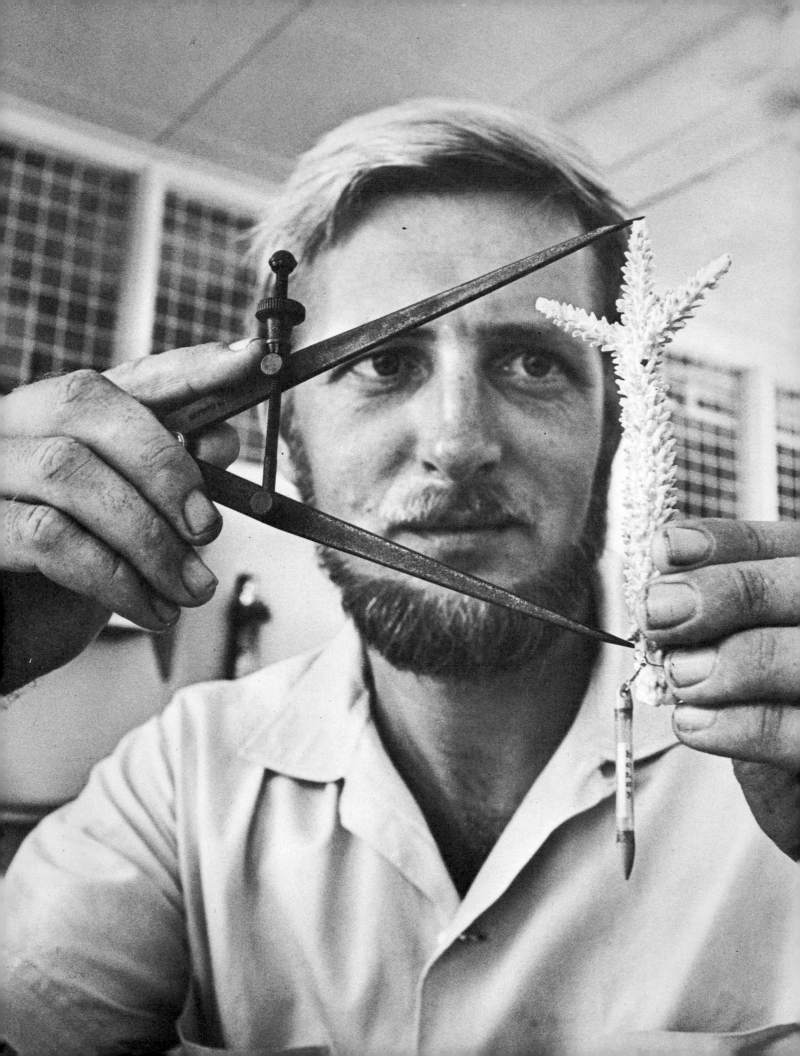

Each moment of discovery
    is part of our aliveness
        with that life
which
        forever impels
        us to go further,
continuing our own evolution—

Totally absorbed moments—
  caught
    pulled out of ourselves
    recreated . . .

Face to face
  with a presence
    at work in us
whose hidden significance
  we have often
    not realized.

29

God-with-us
   is
      inner liberation,
a happening
   in moments of feeling
      something is just right.

We are most human
    (and most divine)
        when standing at the edge
           unsatisfied . . .
ourselves a taking-off point

Absorbed
in the unfolding creativity
that is
God-with-us.

Even
    celebrating God
        with our hands.

Touching
  God-with-us
    in creative loving

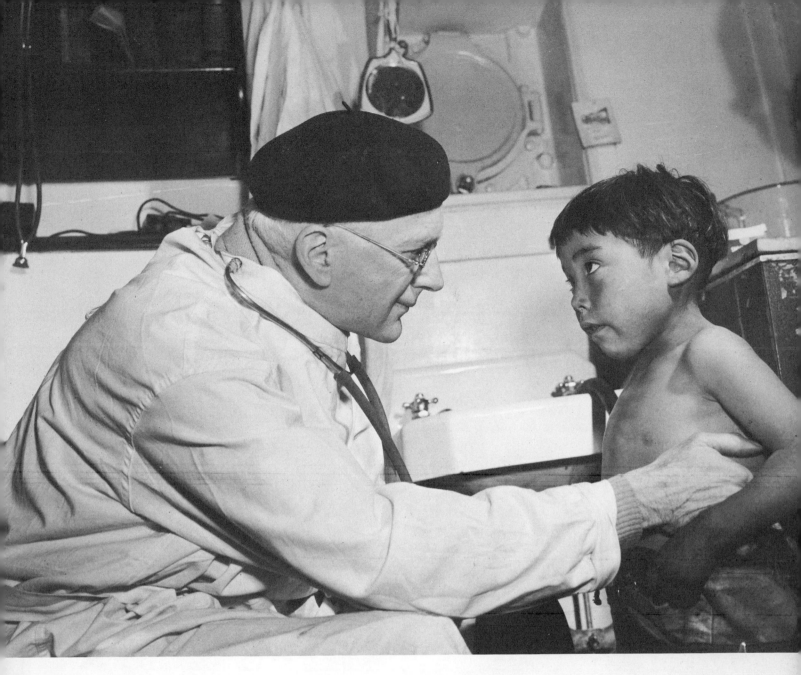

35

"For God is love . . ." (1 John 4:8)

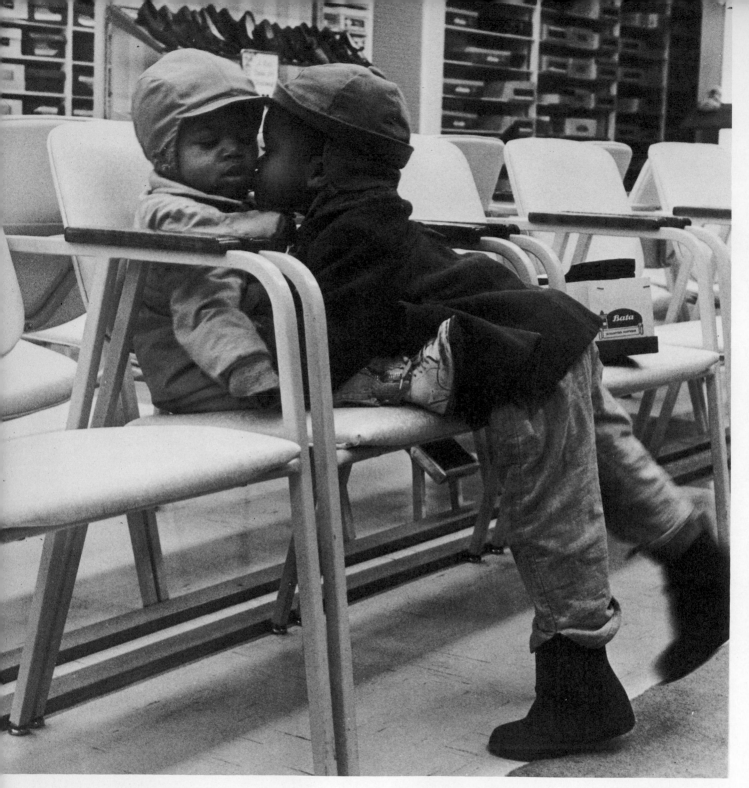

Passing on
    the gift we have become . . .

Sinking into life
to come more alive.

God is as close to us
  as we can risk being close
    to
      our real selves.

The Bible tells of man
    made in the image and likeness
      of God before revealing that
God is a community—
    a three-in-oneness—
      and the life of God
is a community life,
    a life of person-to-person.
      No one becomes a person alone.

We are all a community presence—
    an extension
      of the loving open community—or
      the rejecting closed community—
    that has made us what we are.

GOD IS A LOVING COMMUNITY

God-with-us
    is a personal "Community Presence."
We touch this God most deeply
    in our self-discovery
      as persons
within a loving community.

God-with-us
    can be as personal an experience
as our experience
    of loving and being loved—
      of being 'fully alive'
in a human community.

That is why
 God is as close to us
  as we can risk being close
to our real selves.

> *"Anyone who loves me will heed what I*
> *say: then my Father will love him,*
> *and we will come to him and make our*
> *dwelling with him . . ." (John 14:23)*

Love is the extension of God's community
 into the world,
  into us.

It is the life that makes us more human
 fleshed into the heart
  of our growing sense
of a positive
 personal identity.

Revelation
 appears from within—
  the experience of ourselves
as a community expression
 of love
  that is human—
and divine.

> *"Dwell in my love. If you*
> *heed my commandments, you will dwell*
> *in my love, as I have heeded my*
> *Father's commands and dwell in his*
> *love." (John 15:9–10)*

God is not with-us
      as an invisible person
            dwelling
in those we know and love . . .

. . . but as a
   life
      we share with one another.

We touch
    God-with-us
        in creating human community . . .

. . . in consecrated moments
    sacred to
        life-giving . . .

    "the world is charged
    with the grandeur of God."

    and
the grandeur of God
    is man
        fully alive.

As the search
    for meaning
        continues to unfold
            in human history,
man's quest for God
    will celebrate
        the good news
of just such experiences
    as those
        pictured in this book . . .

Fascination
    creativity
        going one step beyond
succeeding where all odds
    are against us
        probing for answers
to all the questions life puts to us.

Men will recognize
   that they are most deeply involved with
      God
when they touch the world around them
   as invitation—
      and respond with a confident
"Amen."

To believe in God-with-us
   is to find the divine presence
within our own conscious
   responsible
      and free commitment
to become more human.

Faith
   means something as clear and beautiful
as living close to our potential
   for love and creativity,
joyously releasing these
   into the world around us
      believing
that this
   is
      God-with-us.

Ourselves
   a source of life,
      advancing
"... *the fullness of him who fills*
all in all." (*Ephesians 1:23*)

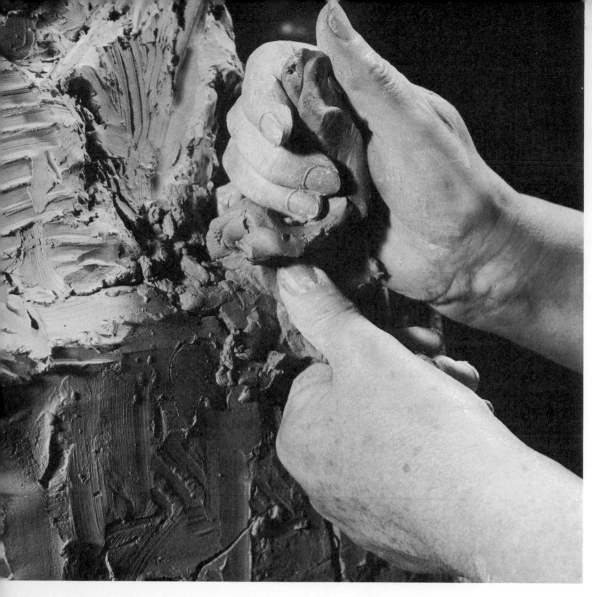

45

*"The Word became flesh and dwelt
among us . . ." (John 1:14)*

The Word was more willing to become
   flesh than we—

The Word was more willing to become
   life than we—

The Word was more willing to become
   love than we—

Flesh
   life
      love

Not gifts from God—
   but God-with-us.

We must learn to touch
   flesh
     life
       love
  from the inside—
recognizing them
  for what they really are.

*". . . all of man's industrial efforts,
all his computations and calculations,
all the nights spent over working
draughts and blueprints, invariably
culminate in the production of a
thing whose sole and guiding principle
is the ultimate principle of simplicity . . .*

*"It is as if there were a natural law
which ordained that to achieve this
end, to refine the curve of a piece
of furniture, or a ship's keel, or
the fuselage of an airplane, until
gradually it partakes of the
elementary purity of the curve of a
human breast or shoulder, there must
be the experimentation of several
generations of craftsmen. In anything
at all, perfection is finally attained
not when there is no longer anything
to add, but when there is no longer
anything to take away, when a body has
been stripped down to its nakedness . . .*

*"There is an ancient myth about the image
asleep in the block of marble until it
is carefully disengaged by the sculptor.
The sculptor must himself feel that he
is not so much inventing or shaping
the curve of breast or shoulder as
delivering the image from its prison."*
                  (Antoine de Saint-Exupéry)

Nothing is changed—
    the curve of the human shoulder
      is the same.

The shore
  line
    still stretches before us.

And yet,
  the kingdom of God
    is at hand—

PLEASE TOUCH.

PHOTO CREDITS

All photos are taken from the collection of the *National Film Board of Canada*, Still Photography Division, Ottawa, Ontario.

1	O. Buck	24	R. Jones
2	Michael Semak	25	John Reeves
3	George Hunter	26	Chris Lund
4	John Reeves	27	Chris Lund
5	Terry Pearce	28	John Reeves
6	Michael Semak	29	John Reeves
7	Joan Latchford	30	Orban
8	Chris Lund	31	Gar Lunney
9	Lutz Dille	32	Ted Grant
10	Gar Lunney	33	Ron Solomon
11	Ted Grant	34	John Reeves
12	Crombie McNeill	35	George Hunter
13	Gar Lunney	36	Ted Grant
14	Crombie McNeill	37	Michael Semak
15	Michael Semak	38	Michael Semak
16	Pierre Gaudard	39	Michael Semak
17	Chris Lund	40	André Le Coz
18	Chris Lund	41	Chuck Diven
19	Chris Lund	42	Bob Brooks
20	Chris Lund	43	Michael Semak
21	Ulrich Marotz	44	Joan Latchford
22	John Ough	45	Gar Lunney
23	Michael Semak	46	Chris Lund

Edwin M. McMahon and Peter A. Campbell
are presently completing doctoral research
in Religious Psychology at the University
of Ottawa. Both are Roman Catholic
priests and well known from their lectures,
retreats and workshops in the United States
and Canada. Their two previously published
books are: *Becoming a Person in the Whole
Christ* and *The In-Between: Evolution
in Christian Faith.*